FIRST
WE EAT,
then we do
EVERYTHING ELSE.

M.F.K. FISHER

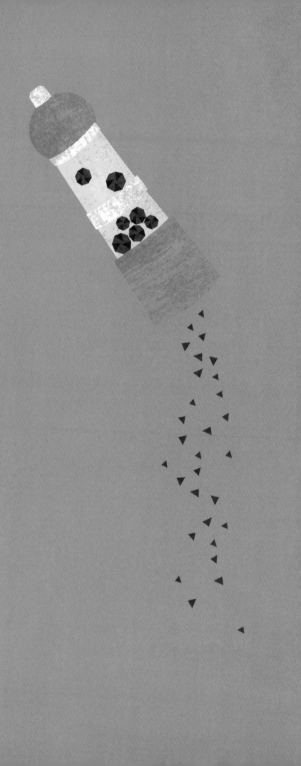

FOOD

xxx is our xxx

COMMON
GROUND,
A UNIVERSAL
EXPERIENCE.

• JAMES BEARD •

— I SEE —

NO PURPOSE IN
BAD COFFEE,
BAD WINE, OR
INSINCERE FRIENDS.

➡ ED MORSE

...you should
CONDUCT
yourself
IN LIFE
—— as at a ——
FEAST.

· EPICTETUS ·

TELL ME
what you eat,
and I will tell you
WHAT YOU ARE.

◆

**ANTHELME
BRILLAT-SAVARIN**

LAUGHTER
is brightest
———— where ————
FOOD IS BEST.

• IRISH PROVERB •

IT'S DIFFICULT
TO THINK
anything but
pleasant thoughts
while eating a
HOMEGROWN
TOMATO.

LEWIS GRIZZARD

DINNER IS NOT
what you do in the evening
• before you do •
something else.
DINNER IS THE
EVENING.

• ART BUCHWALD •